Designs in Wood

Designs in Wood
Paul Bridge and Austin Crossland

Frederick A. Praeger, *Publishers*
New York · Washington

BOOKS THAT MATTER

Published in the United States of America in 1969
by Frederick A. Praeger, Inc., Publishers
111 Fourth Avenue, New York, N. Y. 10003

Library of Congress Catalog Card Number: 77-95270

Printed in Denmark by F. E. Bording Ltd.

Contents

Acknowledgment The authors wish to thank past and present students of Penistone Grammar School who have loaned work for reproduction in the book, also Roy Wragg, Crafts Master, Holmfirth Secondary School, and Ian D. Childs, Crafts Master, Penistone Grammar School, and Ian Barrow.

We can define 'design' as being the process whereby something is planned to fulfil a definite requirement. The considerations involved in the design of an artefact must therefore include all the facets needed to make it successful. These will be (a) the completed article must satisfactorily perform the work for which it is intended, (b) it must be made from the most suitable material, (c) it must be well made so that it can continue to function and (d) it must look and feel right.

The word 'design' is in common use today, sometimes giving rise to the idea that it is of comparatively recent origin, but this can be readily disproved by reference to the tools of early times which are seen in museums. The vessels and weapons are a testimony to man's awareness of the necessity to equip himself to search effectively for food and to defend himself from his enemies in order to exist. The tools were made from the best available material, they were made so well that in use they were reliable and, additionally, they appeared and felt right thus satisfying man's sensitivity.

Historical study shows that the weighting given to these criteria is occasionally used in ways which reveal that a true understanding of its nature, its possibilities and its limitations is lacking and thus it has not been used to best advantage. The best results should be achieved when the characteristics of the material have been fully investigated and perhaps new tools designed to deal with it; sometimes an over-exuberance in their use has led to an exhibition of technical skill which tends to violate the nature of the material. Whilst such craft skill may well excite admiration there is the danger of some loss in sensitivity for the material. Rather should the tool be regarded as a means to an end instead of being an end in itself. Method of use seems less important than the realisation that the tool can be used to give practical form to an idea. When is the most satisfactory stage reached? Perhaps when much experience in the use of the material leads to restraint when working it, with consequent reliance on its natural qualities.

Man's creative nature leads him to attempt to make progress which in turn demands experiment. In this context it would seem that to copy what has gone before is a retrograde step leading to stagnation and therefore we feel that to be completely successful with woodwork the articles we make should be from our own ideas and that they should take on solid form with all the skill we can muster. Obviously these two factors will vary with the individual, but we believe that their development should proceed side by side so that the likelihood of stagnation of either is minimised.

If we agree that design and production go hand in hand, we must commence by learning design as well as techniques. To put our objectives into perspective we would put creativity first with the techniques of tool manipulation a means to this end.

We would impress on the reader that, intentionally, some of the sections have not been dealt with in depth for much information is already available on techniques, timbers, glues and finishes. Our aim is not that this book should be a manual of instruction but more of an encouragement to maintain a constant attitude of enquiry and investigation. The sections named are touched upon because they are an integral part of the design process and it is not possible to design without giving them due consideration.

Visual form

In the initial stages it is probably a good idea not to make functional objects but to do research, and experiment with shapes, textures, patterns and form. Everything that we create, whether it is written, painted or constructed is based on our experiences and the danger in early efforts of designing everyday functional artefacts is that our experiences are so limited that we revert to copying what other people have created, without the knowledge of how these solutions were achieved. If we concentrate on simply experimenting with the tools, with the materials and with pattern and form, then we should be much more free in our approach, and when we eventually have to design functional objects these will be based on our knowledge of shapes and materials, and not on other people's experiences.

When we consider the visual aspects of design we are concerned with putting things into order because for man to function efficiently he must put his things in order. His suits go in a wardrobe, his shirts go in drawers, his papers go in pigeon holes and because of his need for order so his visual surroundings need an order—an order of form and pattern and texture.

Here we have a muddle without any order. We can see no harmony or relationship in the shapes themselves or the areas surrounding them and so it is disturbing and we get a feeling of unrest...

These shapes do not relate to each other, neither do the surrounding shapes.

If we select shapes of a similar form we feel happier because here is a beginning of an order. But although they are in the same family we are still not satisfied because they are not arrnged in any apparent order but appear to be scattered haphazardly.

Here the order is far more obvious, everything is of the same family and everything balances. But the spacing is so obviously even that it becomes monotonous and so we require a form that balances without monotony.

Visual balance is appreciated because we can relate this to mechanical balance as with the weighing scales shown diagrammatically.

In this grouping we can still create a balance but without monotony for each area is different and our eyes can travel around without being bored.

When we consider the visual aspects of design we are concerned with putting things into a visual order. We have to use shapes and materials which relate to each other, we have to consider balance and movement, harmony and discord, patterns and shapes, negative and positive.

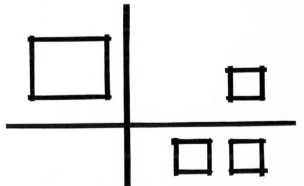

Before we commence to construct an object in timber it would be as well to investigate the possibilities revolving round a simple rectangular form. We can take a simple geometric unit and repeat it

1 Repeat unit at right angles and at varying angles

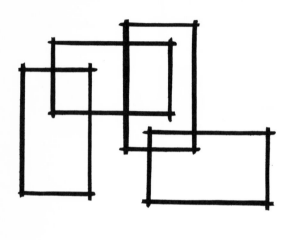

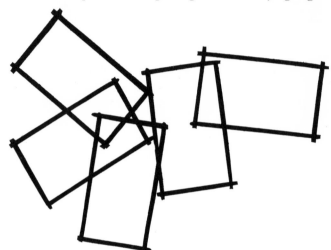

2 Varying sizes and repeating at right angles and at varying angles

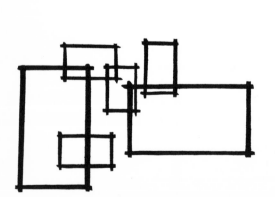

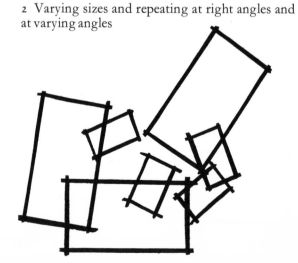

3 Changing form by first adjusting one side, then another, etc, and each adjustment considered as a new form

4 Dissect rectangle and reassemble as a different form

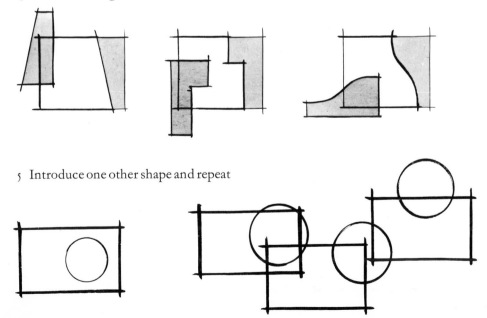

5 Introduce one other shape and repeat

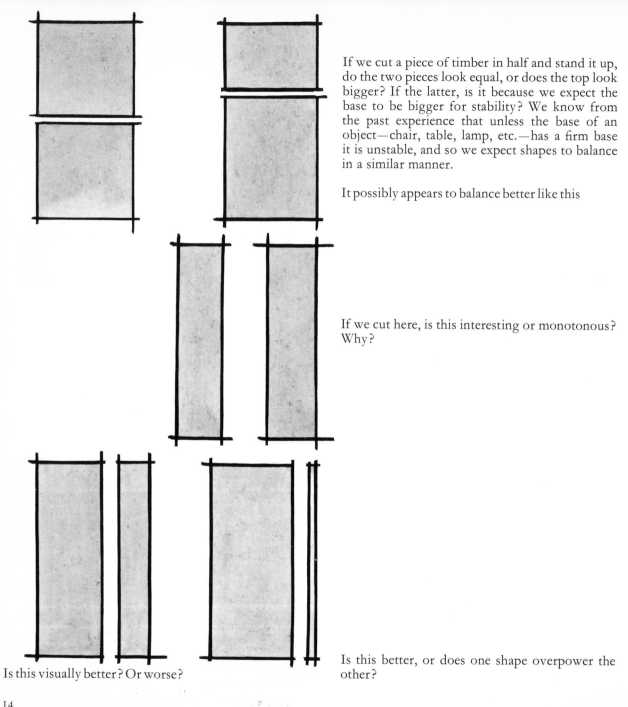

If we cut a piece of timber in half and stand it up, do the two pieces look equal, or does the top look bigger? If the latter, is it because we expect the base to be bigger for stability? We know from the past experience that unless the base of an object—chair, table, lamp, etc.—has a firm base it is unstable, and so we expect shapes to balance in a similar manner.

It possibly appears to balance better like this

If we cut here, is this interesting or monotonous? Why?

Is this visually better? Or worse?

Is this better, or does one shape overpower the other?

When we start relating one or more shapes together other visual problems arise, for instance we create movements.

One piece of timber, because of the grain and the proportion, has a visual movement towards its length.

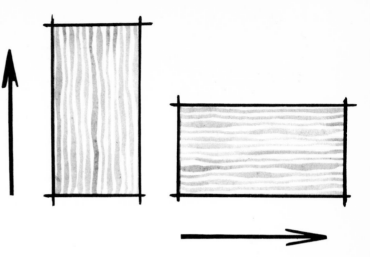

If we put the two together we get these movements.

Here we are using the grain to help us.

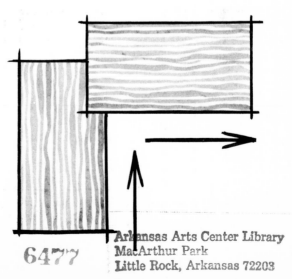

15

Here the grain and the shape help.

Here neither the shape of timber nor its grain help, but we can still produce an apparent movement.

Experiments which involve putting timber into an order.

At this stage these are mainly two dimensional.

All these experiments are relative. If we consider one area of card or wood we can discuss its merits in relation to (a) itself or (b) to its surroundings.

In the case of a rectangle
(a) We have to consider its length in relation to its width if it is two dimensional. But if it is a solid, we have a third dimension to take into consideration.
(b) When we think of a shape in relation to its surroundings then this is much more complex, and a shape which is basically right as a proportion may have to be adjusted when related to other shapes, other colours, other textures.

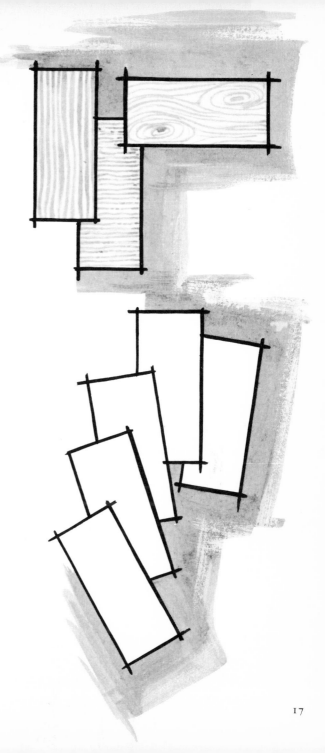

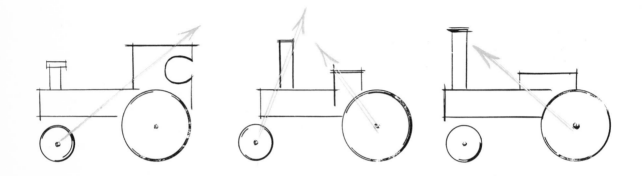

The transition to three dimension can be made by referring to simple toys. In constructing simple toys we can demonstrate some of the requirements in design. We mentioned choosing shapes which had similar family characteristics and we also discussed balance and movements and all these can readily be seen in this model steam roller.

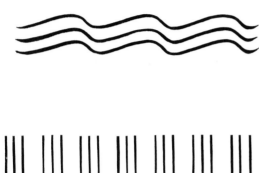

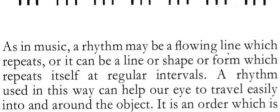

As in music, a rhythm may be a flowing line which repeats, or it can be a line or shape or form which repeats itself at regular intervals. A rhythm used in this way can help our eye to travel easily into and around the object. It is an order which is readily understood.

We tend to think that rhythm, movement, etc, are only contained in 'works of art' but this of course is not true, they are in everything we see around us.

In these toy lorries we can see simple examples of repeat rhythms and simple directional movements.

Influence of tools and materials

If we are to work in timber then it is essential that we know something about the material, and although we can learn a great deal from books and from listening to people talk about wood and watching other people work with wood, the only way in which we can really understand the working properties of timber is for us to work in the material ourselves. Initially if we make simple objects in wood we can discover the difference in grain, textures, etc, and we begin to understand its possibilities and appreciate its limitations. Also whilst we do this we should construct objects which tax our visual senses as well as taxing us physically and mentally. To be able to construct an object in a material it is essential that we know and appreciate the material itself. We must also understand the methods whereby we can shape and form the material and also we must realise the possibilities within the material from the visual point of view. All these criteria must go together. We cannot really work in wood if we do not know its possibilities, or if we do not understand how to shape it; nor can we be successful if the objects we make lack a visually sensitive approach to the material.

Basically we can utilise timber by (a) cutting away (b) building up, by fastening together two or more pieces (c) bending. Let us first consider (a). Immediately we cut a piece of wood in two, or if we cut an area of timber away, so the form of the wood changes and so also does the space around it. It is essential that we should appreciate this change and it is also essential that we should see the significance of such a change and what it means to us visually.

It is also essential that the use of tools and the making of objects is thought provoking and must be treated in an enquiring and creative manner. We must at all times be questioning the type of tool required and also be considering how it is best to use this chosen tool. So we are continually setting ourselves problems:

1 We need to cut this timber here, what tool will cut it best?
2 Why is this?
3 How shall we hold the tool?
4 Why do we hold it thus?
5 How do we hold the work?
6 Is it possible we could use the tool differently?
7 Is it possible the tool could be improved?
The following information on the use of tools is merely a guide and should not stop us questioning the choice of tool or the methods employed.

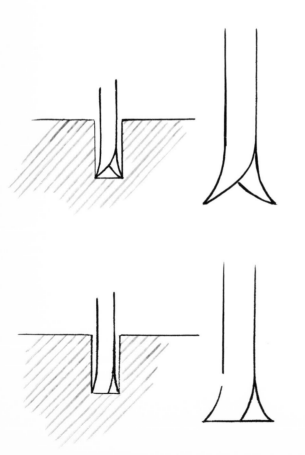

Cutting

Tool technique is an integral part of the artefact design process and must be mentioned. The design of saw teeth for cutting across the grain of wood ensures that the fibres are severed by knife-like points. Waste wood is pushed away by the rest of the tooth leaving a surface of rough texture, the degree of roughness dependent upon kind of timber.

Cutting along or with the grain involved a different action—more of a tearing one with a chisel-like edge severing the fibres, and again the remainder of the tooth carrying away the waste leaving a rough texture with stringy edges.

Skill with the tenon saw is probably the greatest time-saving factor for the worker in wood. The acquisition of this skill is wholly dependent on practice and one or two pointers may assist the beginner. Stance is important, with the body well balanced on feet fairly wide apart. Supporting the wood on a bench-hook, the user should begin the cut on the edge farthest from him. Using long strokes with little weight applied he should attempt to keep his body—with the exception of the arm—quite still throughout the sawing process. Moving the body, and particularly the head, from side to side, greatly hinders the development of sawing skill. With the large frame saw, commonly used in Denmark, in place of our type of tenon saw, it is difficult to see over the large frame and so most users maintain a natural stance with the head kept still. This may account for the high degree of skill shown by Danish children in the use of a saw which appears particularly unwieldy.

Cutting guide with plastic laminate insert to reduce wear.

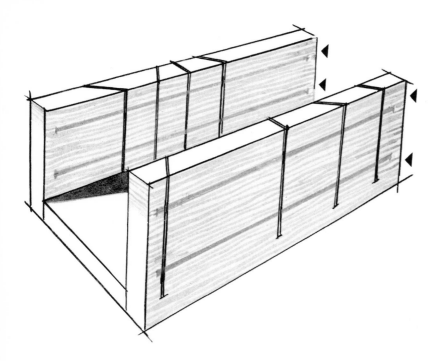

The beginner may find a mitre box with a cross-cutting guide, of some assistance, but he should not become wholly dependent upon it for it is too narrow to hold timber of wide dimensions.

For cutting shaped work, the coping saw is effective, the important point concerning its use being that tension must always be maintained by ensuring that the teeth point towards the user. Effective cutting is possibe only if the work is supported close to the saw; this require the frequent adjustment of the position of the work in the vice.

Shaping with chisel and gouge. The firmer chisel is a potentially dangerous tool if used experimentally without discussion and thought. The necessity for firmly securing the wood to be worked can be realised by attempting to use a 1 inch (25,4 mm) firmer chisel with one hand on wood held by the other hand. For the first work the bench vice is perhaps most suitable, giving a positive grip to wood of parallel width or thickness. Analysis of the chisel action shows that the knife-like edge severs wood fibres cleanly, leaving, in contrast to the saw, a smooth texture. The material exerts an influence here, demanding that the worker be prepared to change the direction of his chisel; each side of the tool will be found to be

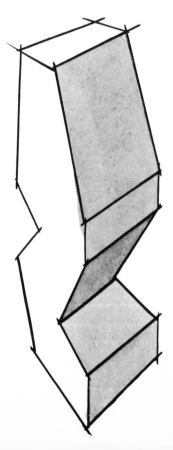

suited to different shapes, the flat more efficient on convex curves and the sharpened on concave surfaces. Holding the chisel with both hands resting on the work or vice, to assist the chisel in its slicing action, is safe and effective.

Experimental work by these handparing methods can be followed by deep cutting using a mallet; wood structure and grain peculiarities will be encountered and possibilities and limitations discovered.

In these exercises we have attempted to create movements and negative and positive forms. Also we have placed pieces in relation to one another.

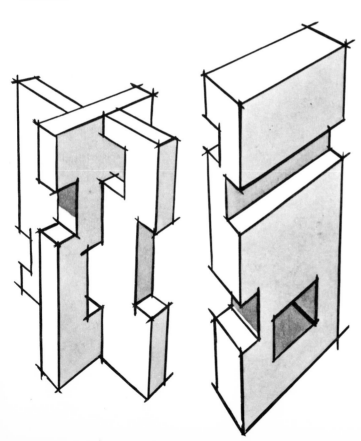

Form planning

To work in wood can be a comparatively slow process and one in which, if a mistake is made, rectification is not easy. Before an artefact is begun, therefore, pre-planning on paper is advisable. This is cheap, the process is quick and lends itself well to experimentation and, although the shapes may require modification when seen three-dimensionally, decisions of the form the work is to assume should be made before the work on the timber is begun. Following experimental work with a mallet and chisel a small bowl or dish could be a useful exercise, a curved chisel i.e. firmer gouge being added to the tool range.

Initially a dish would be planned by deciding on its purpose, where it would be used and any other considerations necessary according to special circumstances. This would give an indication of size and form within certain limits but would leave much to be decided concerning form, space and surface treatment. If a start is made with a rectangular piece of timber, experiments can be made by cutting areas away, but to repeat what has been previously stated, initial experiments on paper are to be preferred. Dozens or perhaps hundreds of pieces of paper or cards could be cut to the same scale as the timber and slow and systematic experiment made with possible shapes. Only by having many shapes available can the relative merits and faults be discussed and assessed and a store of information built up as a personal library from which to develop future designs.

This method can give a good idea of how the final object will look, but during the making process careful observation and study may make modification necessary if the three-dimensional forms on the wood grain dictate a change.

Can we extract one shape as being better than the others and then develop it further?

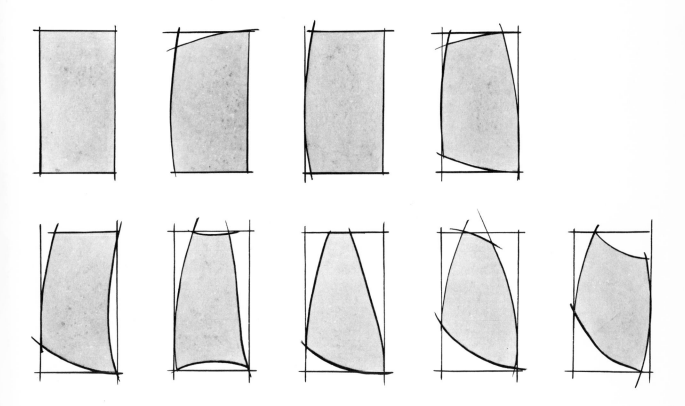

Has this gone too far? Have we destroyed the original shape? Possibly we need to retrace our steps and develop along another avenue.

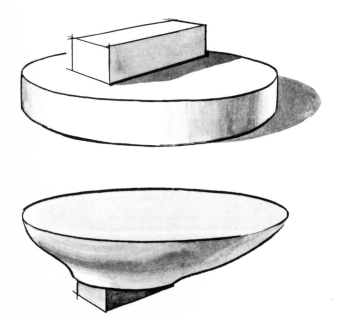

If we develop form and space in this way, we can begin to appreciate shapes which strike us as being better than others. If we are going to gain knowledge, and if we are going to be able to use this information in the future, we must try to define *why* one shape succeeds and one fails, and *why* this shape is better and this one worse. It is not enough to say 'we like it'. We must try to define *why* we like it. If we can say why one shape is superior to another we can develop the better parts in further sketches or models. Also, if we can decide that some proportions or shapes are inferior, these could be eliminated in further development. In this way we can deelop a library of visual experiences and a foundation on which other experiments can be based.

The method of constantly questioning during planning continues during making. How can the shape be best marked on to the wood? How can the surplus wood be removed quickly and accurately? How will the dish be held during making and which part will be cut first and why? Answers may be that pasting a paper shape on to a suitable sized block followed by cutting with saw and smoothing by spokeshave are valid methods for solving the first problem, but the holding of the work and which part to cut first and why, are so closely dependent on each other that they must be solved together.

The difficulty of securing a hollowed object whilst working on some part of it suggests that hollowing be the last process, so the decision is made to cut the outer surface first and to hold the dish blank by gluing a softwood block to the centre of what is selected as the upper or hollow surface.

What size should the block be? It has to secure the work so that the dish does not break away on the glue line when a heavy blow is given to the gouge. This usually means a block of substantial size.

Cutting of the outer surface having been completed, the holding block can be sawn off and re-glued to the centre of what is now the completed base.

How can smoothness be achieved after the use of gouge and mallet? A curved scraper or one improvised from a broken H.S.S. power hacksaw blade by grinding can help, with glasspaper used after damping the scraped surface and allowing it to dry. How will the work be given a permanent finish? The holding block can be carefully sawn off, the base dressed with a smoothing plane and the polish selected according to the kind of finish required for the particular function of the dish, its situation or surroundings, and its appearance. Perhaps smoothness and freedom from irregularity is not suited to the timber selected and a wire brushed texture is what the nature of the material suggests.

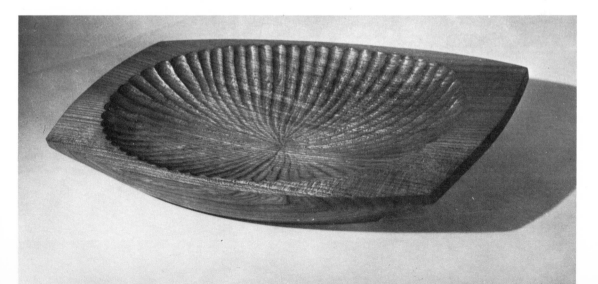

Design method

The design process is seen emphatically to be not added decoration but the whole exercise of conceiving and making an artefact. It is the method of selecting and rejecting, experimenting and testing, so that each stage is thoroughly covered and the finished article will function correctly and be visually an acceptable part of the environment for which it is intended.

The process involves

1 Stating the problem precisely.
2 Collecting all relevant information.
3 Studying and sieving that information.
4 Decisions on materials, methods and form of the whole and of component parts.
5 Experimentation and testing including model making.
6 Production of prototype.

A design for a stool can be a relatively simple exercise but it still requires meticulous analysis of detail in setting out the design brief. If the problem is 'to design a stool', the first requirement would seem to be to eliminate, if possible, pre-conceived ideas on stools and to concentrate on the basic essentials.

The essential function is to support a human being, but a stool for use at a bar will be very different from a stool needed by a child whilst watching television.

The design brief has thus to be far more precise and can be more exactly worded through asking a series of questions and determining answers. Why? What? When? Who? Where? How? may all be needed for some examples but most will be applicable for the majority of problems.

Why is the stool required?
What will the stool be used for?
When will it be used?
Where will it be used?
Who will use it?

The close investigation of the brief should lead to a more satisfactory solution to the problem.

The next stage, since the article is for human use, must involve considerations related to human anatomy, the way in which it moves, where support is needed and how large an area of support is needed. The obvious way to find this out is to try sitting on objects of varying heights and to note reactions. At the same time it may be possible to experiment with areas of seat, texture of seat, and type of support.

Although there are books which do supply such information it is much better if we discover these details for ourselves so that we fully understand our finding.

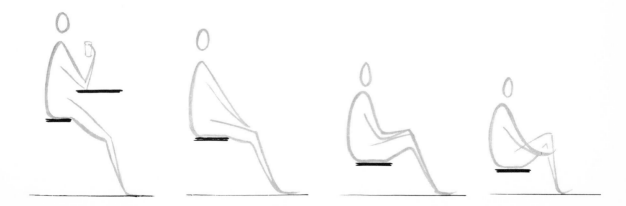

Having discovered this information it should be possible to evolve ways in which the seat may be supported at the determined height from the floor. If the stool has to be freely movable, suspending the seat from walls or ceiling can be discarded, and the endless variety of ways in which it may be supported from the floor can be investigated.

The choice of underframe is closely allied to the type of material used and also the methods of construction, and we cannot decide on one frame, simply because it looks good, if we have not also considered the most suitable material and the constructional details. Conversely, we cannot decide to use a certain joint unless the form has been considered. All these things must be developed together. Nothing should be discarded until *proved* to be of no value and nothing assumed to be correct until substantiated.

It can be seen that this careful consideration of all the problems is not only essential when making objects, but is also necessary when we go out to buy an article. If we consider everything in this way then we can be sure that articles we buy are completely suitable for our needs both functionally and visually.

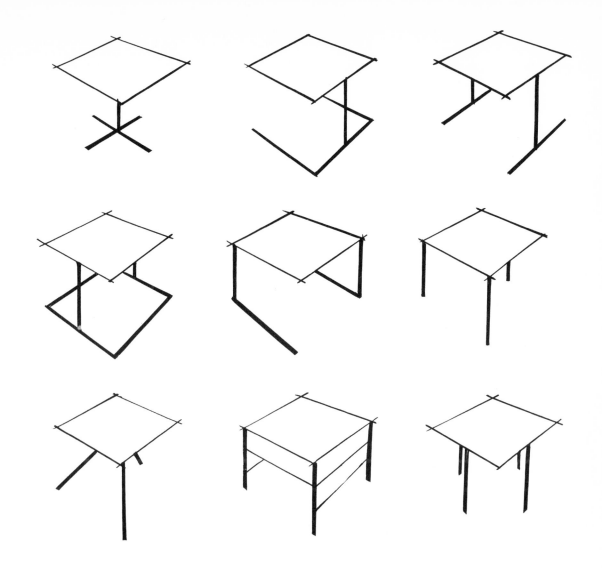

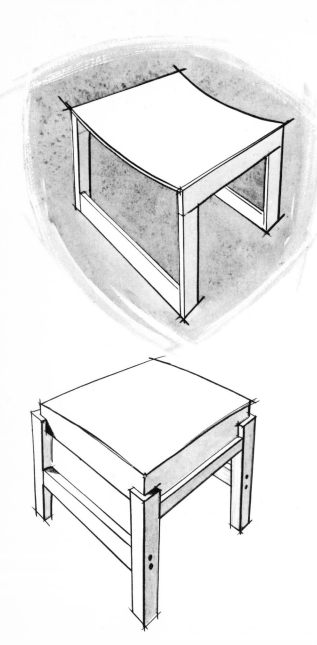

The stool is normally only used for a short time and is basically a seat held at a given distance above the ground and therefore allows plenty of scope for many solutions.

It can take many forms and be constructed in many different ways. The final solution should be considered as a prototype as it should lead us to consider other possibilities. Variations and improvements can be incorporated in further experiments.

Interesting visual use of 'Knock Down' fittings which were machined from stainless steel. The stool is blockboard and finished in melamine wood finish.

The design formula, as suggested for the stool, can also be adopted for any other article; but each and any object will require complete appraisal in order to ensure that no requirement is overlooked. A chair is much more complicated and many considerations need to be studied.

We can only discover sizes and angles, areas of support, stresses and strains, by relating our researches to the human figure; this analysis should provide information with regard to height, width, length and angle of back. We should also know whether or not arms and head supports are necessary.

Although there are British Standards for the sizes of angles of some chairs, it would seem that we can gain more information by experimenting and discovering the facts for ourselves. Then having reached our own conclusions we can check with British Standards to see if our findings tally with theirs.

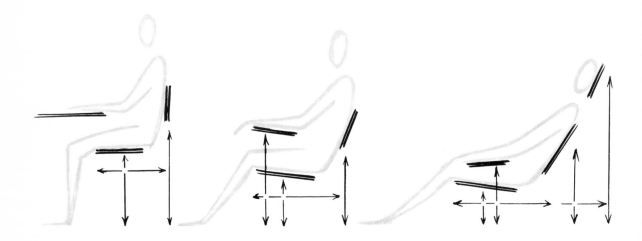

We have now discovered where we require support and also the sizes and angles of these supports.

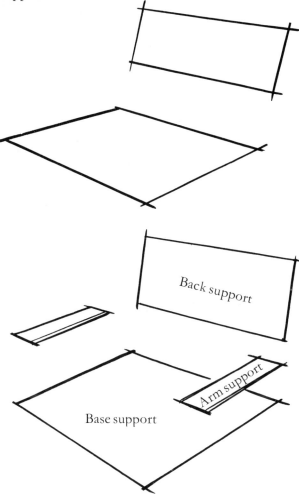

Back support

Arm support

Base support

All these supports require fastening together and holding at a comfortable distance from the floor.

These requirements can be developed in an endless variety of shapes including linking all the supports together.

Means of holding the seat, back and arm rests
together.

Providing we have developed a feeling for design, this can be largely a personal choice, but must be based on an appreciation of form, space, construction, material, etc, and should also be based on environment, for what looks right in one setting can look incongruous in another. A beautiful Chippendale chair could look out of place among modern furniture in a modern house.

The solution can be as simple as this:
or as complicated as this seventeenth century chair

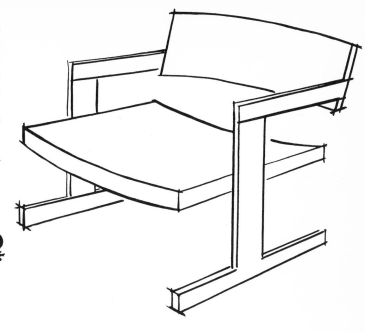

The main function of a chair is that it must be comfortable to sit on but it must also look right.

It has long been an opinion that if an object functions properly then it is bound to look right, but this is not necessarily so. When it does happen, it is because consciously or unconsciously the builder of the article did consider aesthetics and also his knowledge of his materials and construction was such that he did not violate their character.

Both these chairs are quite functional and, in their own period and environment, considered quite good in appearance.

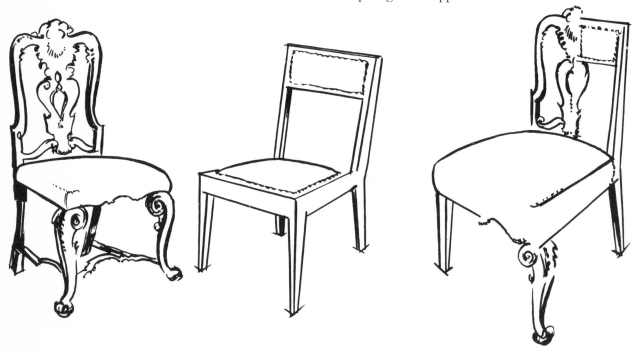

But what happens here:

The chair is still functional, it is still just as stable, as well made, and as comfortable to sit on— but does it look right?

So we are *very* concerned with appearances.

Shapes made by cutting wood away, as in the seventeenth century chair, can draw attention from the natural qualities of the material when displayed as an unbroken true area but to produce such a really flat surface the cutting needs rigid control. The chisel in a jig was the logical step in tool design in order to accomplish this, and the result was the plane.

Types of plane and their design for various purposes are dealt with in many test books. Achieving surfaces on timber which are true and free from tears and chatter marks is a skill acquired fairly quickly on all but the most difficult woods. The latter which may have interlocked grain or simply be particularly hard, need the services of a plane sharpened and set specifically to deal with them. Present day steel planes have the advantages of quick adjustment and blades which can be more than $\frac{1}{8}$ in. (3.2 mm) in thickness. This thin ground and sharpened rapidly since they are little blade tends to chatter when used on hard wood and to remedy this the grinding and sharpening angle needs to be as large as possible, consistent with adequate clearance during use.

The truing of shaped work with a special plane the compass plane will leave a good surface but the size of arc radius with which the plane will deal is limited. For smaller radii the spokeshave will be necessary but this tool has no cap iron to quickly break the shaving in order to reduce the tendency to tear. A slicing action will help and the smallest amount of blade projecting is also advisable.

Surfaces

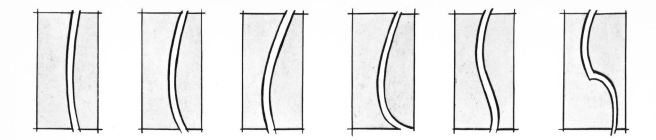

We can shape a block using very flat concave or convex curves, or deeper curves or combinations of curves, and because these shapes are all of the same family we should be able to re-assemble them into a unit which is visually interesting.

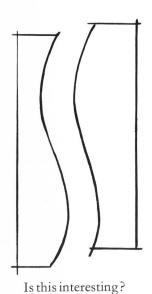

Is this interesting?

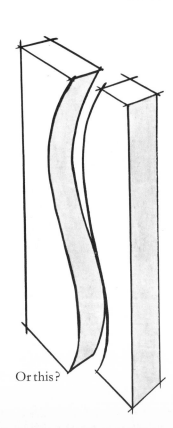

Or this?

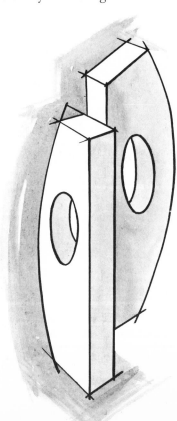

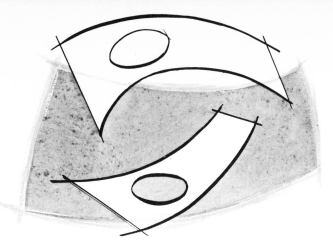

All the shapes here are of the same family because they all comprise the same sort of curve. The spaces also are of the same family and these help to create a movement which revolves around the centre making our eye move outward but also back in again.

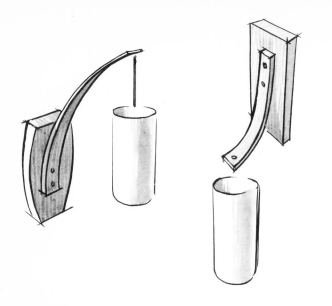

Curved shapes can be created by bending, as opposed to cutting away. Whilst the cross sectional size of timber which can be bent by steaming and securing in shaped jigs, is limiting to the amateur not possessing specialised equipment, it is possible to build up or laminate thick veneers and bend them in the same operation. In place of specialised equpment, home-made jigs can be forged from rejected car spring leaves. The tendency for glue to fail when used on teak or Rio rosewood can be minimised if the veneers are cut on a fine saw and glued quickly before prolonged exposure of the surfaces to air.

The additional strength of a laminated structure can be used to advantage. Experimental curved models can be fairly quickly made from constructional veneer i.e. about $\frac{1}{16}$ in. (1.6 mm) in thickness by heating on a hot tube and exerting gentle hand pressure during the process.

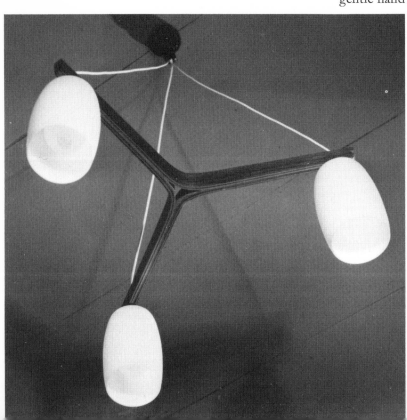

If we examine the requirements of a stand to hold toast, we would need to know the size of a piece of toast. How many pieces of toast may be needed? Will they stand or lie flat? Will the stand be carried or passed around? Will it require cleaning? Where will it be used? Factory? Hotel? Home? What facilities and materials have we available for making a toast rack?

One basic laminate may lead to many solutions.

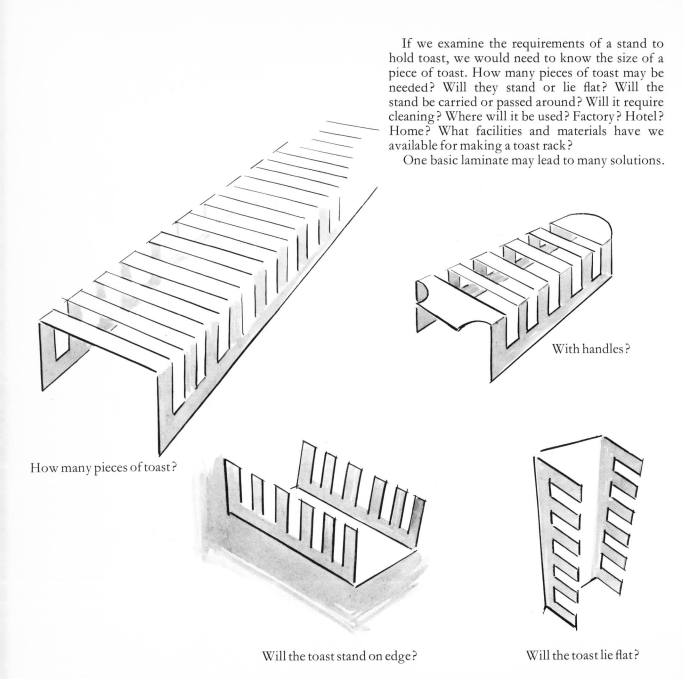

How many pieces of toast?

With handles?

Will the toast stand on edge?

Will the toast lie flat?

We are not limited to simply using laminates, but a laminated structure is very different from a structure created by fabrication.

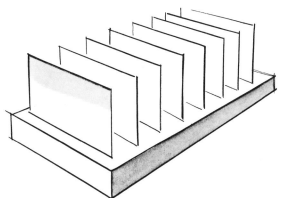

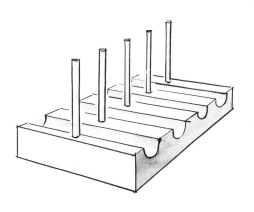

Complete circles can be laminated as in this stool.

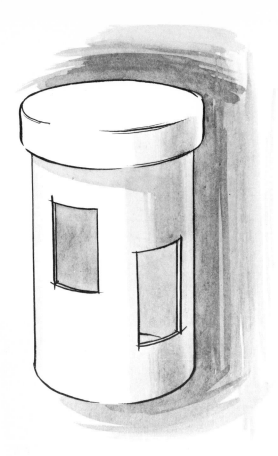

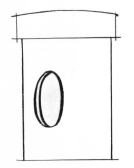 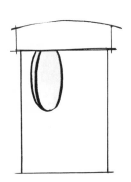 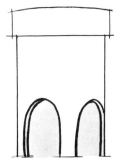 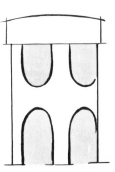

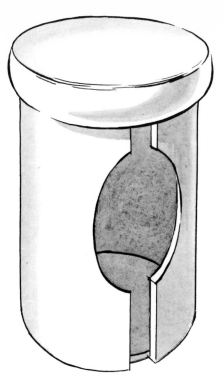

Two half circles

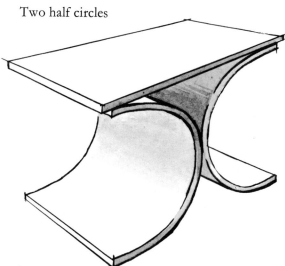

Three part circles

Half circles can make numerous articles—
stools, waste paper boxes, plant troughs, etc

Simple problems in laminates. We can create single curves, convex, concave, double curves, and having laminated we can cut shapes away.

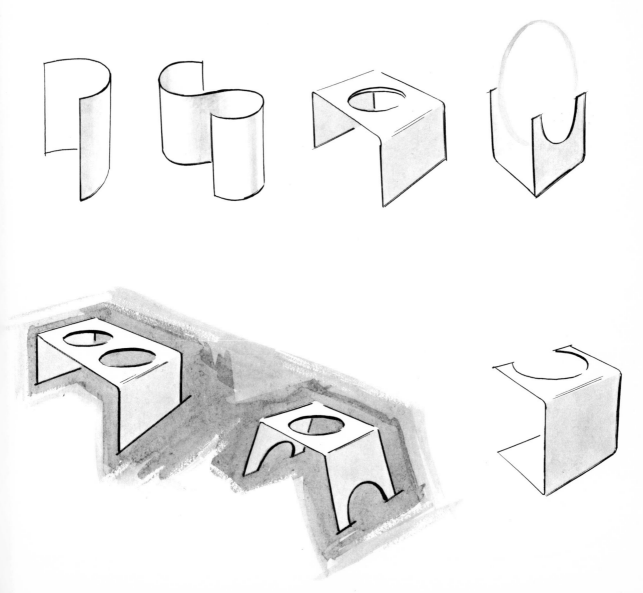

How did we arrive at the proportions for these egg cups? By logical development. Why? What? When? Who? Where?

It can be seen that we are developing a formula for design which may change slightly, depending on the problem but the general procedure is always the same.

Our starting points here appear to be:

(a) The egg, size, shape, weight, etc.

(b) The position the egg is to be held

(c) Where will it be used (an egg cup for a factory canteen is not necessarily the same as an egg cup in a home).

The answers to the queries will present further problems.

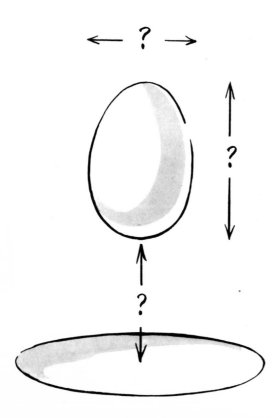

Our ideas should not be limited to only one material or one method of construction. Many of the shapes previously arrived at lend themselves to fabricating.

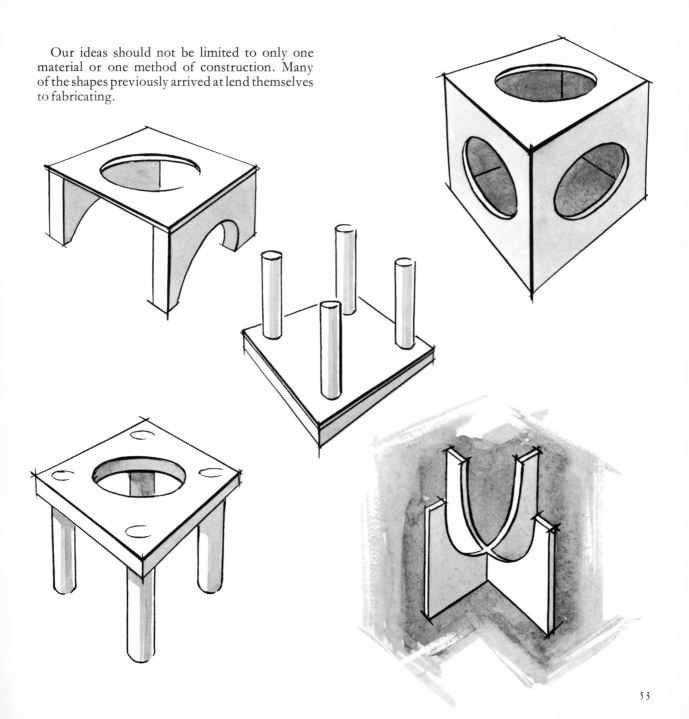

Stacking set

Turned

Portions cut out

This is the block of wood, what can we do to shape it?

How can we carve the timber away?

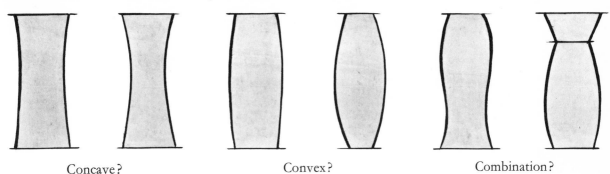

Concave?   Convex?   Combination?

Whatever shape we cut on one side is reproduced on the other. The lathe and tools will also dictate the shape which evolves.

Turning. The process of shaping materials as they rotate against a cutting tool can be strictly controlled by determining the path of the tool in a mechanical way, or it may be freely creative by hand guidance of the tool. Technically, a peeling action is best on most timbers but to achieve a good finish on the more brittle species such as the ebony, a scraping action may be the better way, working in some cases as little as $\frac{1}{8}$ in. (3.2 mm) at a time.

In turning we can create concave and convex forms, full forms and thin lines, but we can carve so much away that we destroy the surface of the timber and completely lose its character.

But of course we are not limited to producing chessmen by turning. The set on this page was created in square section sycamore. The corresponding set was made in Bombay rosewood.

We have discussed mainly the method whereby we can start with a rectangular or circular piece of timber and by adjusting the shape minutely we can assess each form relative to itself or to its surroundings. There are, of course, other ways of arriving at forms and shapes, and our starting point might very well be inspired by natural or man-made forms.

Some shown on this page could well be the beginning but, as will be easily seen when they are all drawn together, they are a jumble and one only may be suitable for selection and development. It is emphasised that to base a wood carving on a pebble form will need much effort to develop since the materials are so different in their nature. To simply re-produce in wood what is good in a pebble may reveal a lack of sensitivity towards materials.

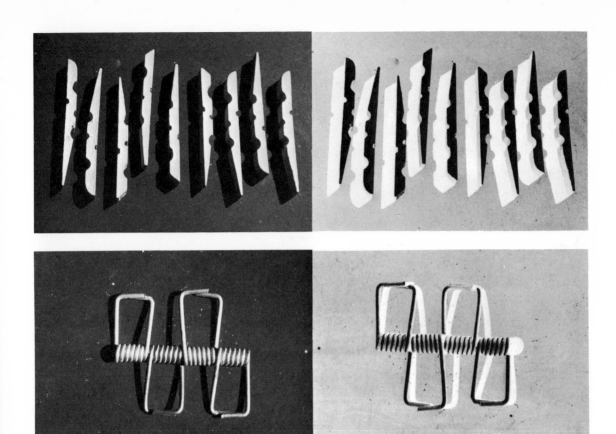

Clothes pegs might also give us an idea for a screen

We can arrange these to create movements, balance, and negative and positive forms.

When we design anything we can only draw on our experiences and on our environment and therefore we must learn to look at our surroundings and analyse everything from a visual point of view.

This type of flat pattern might suggest a motif for a box lid.

A simple box

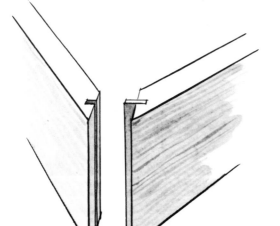

A simple method of box making is to mitre the corners and secure each with a piece of constructional veneer glued into saw cuts.

These serve two purposes; they locate the corners exactly in position and serve as dowels. The mitres can be trued in a home made fixture, using a finely set smoothing plane, and the saw kerfs can be made on the same fixture. Small boxes can be fitted with a top and bottom by simply planting them on using a synthetic resin glue. Operation of the fixture will be clear from the sketch.

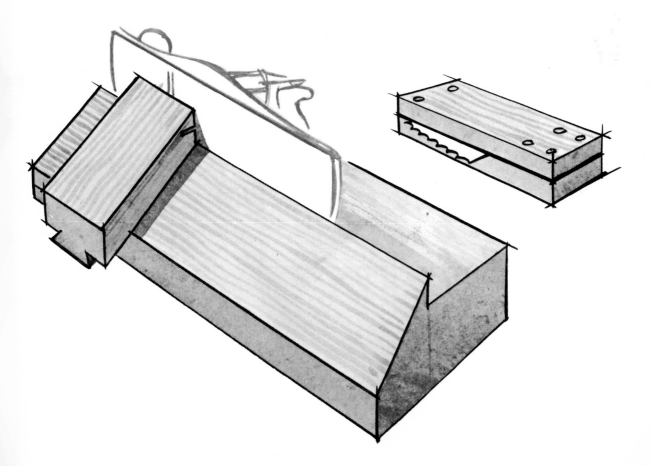

If we are going to create a pattern of holes filled with resin it would be a good idea in the first instance if we limit ourselves to just a few holes and arrange these, bearing in mind the criteria of balance, negative form, movement, monotony, etc.

As this is the lid of a box it would need to be seen from all angles. It must balance from all views.

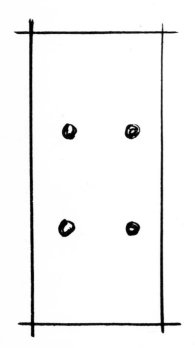

Rather rigid arrangement?

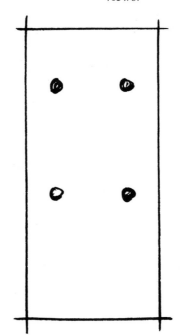

Is this more interesting or not? What is it like upside down?

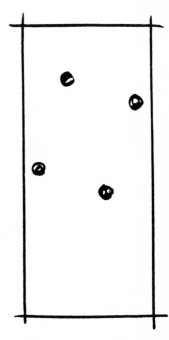

We can create different movements and different spaces by tilting.